# Praise for Jill Talbot's Writing

### *The Way We Weren't: A Memoir*

A magnetic pull sets in while reading *The Way We Weren't*, a sinking into the author's state of heart and mind, a compulsion to keep turning the pages. The memoir's allure is a testament to Jill Talbot's formidable talent.

— *The Boston Globe*

We pay attention to the authors who are able to make their own lives and thoughts vividly present to us. This is what Jill Talbot does, and she does it so well it can be unsettling at times.

— *The Rumpus*

A book of tremendous emotional undercurrents.

— *Los Angeles Review of Books*

Talbot has a remarkable gift for language . . . delectable prose.

— *Brevity*

A beautiful, intimate book.

—*Guernica*

Talbot is fearless in her excavation of the past—as though the future depends on it.

— *Passages North*

### *The Last Year: Essays*

The moments that change us, the ghosts that follow us, the memories that slow us down or keep us afloat – Jill Talbot has found the language for all of that. This is a book about the in-between time, when we look back at multiple beginnings as we brace for the good-bye. Talbot, a longtime single mother, hopes she was enough as she prepares to launch her daughter into the world. Anyone who has ever loved a child will recognize themselves in her mirror. I didn't want this book to end.

— Connie Schultz, Pulitzer Prize-winning author of *The Daughters of Erietown*

In *The Last Year,* Jill Talbot turns the small things sacred, distilling the quiet moments between a mother and daughter into something veering toward revelation. Each page reminds us that the greatest dramas of our lives often go unnoticed—unless we do the noticing. Part epiphany, part elegy, all love. This book is a small mercy. Its gift is grace.

— B.J. Hollars, author of *Go West, Young Man: A Father and Son Rediscover America on the Oregon Trail*

In *The Last Year,* Jill Talbot achieves that rare magic that can exist in the finest examples of the essay form: she captures the ecstatic, mysterious fullness of life in each moment. These missives are about so many things — parenthood, grief, fear, pain, joy, art. Every sentence carries the weight of the past, the breathless potential of the future. Every detail is loaded with honesty, introspection, and, above all else, care. To read it, to bear witness to this mother/daughter relationship as Talbot stands on the precipice of enormous change, is a gift.

— Lucas Mann, author of *Captive Audience: On Love and Reality TV* and *Attachments: Essays on Fatherhood and Other Performances*

Jill Talbot's *The Last Year* is an evocative and heart wrenching portrait of her final days living with her daughter, Indie, who's about to leave home for university – just as the world begins to shut down in the face of the Covid19 pandemic. With penetrating insight and raw honesty, Talbot explores the lingering absent presence of the relationships that shape our lives, from former lovers to deceased parents, as she questions 'What happens after an ending?' Across a series of deftly crafted essays Talbot's prose draws lasting images of a precarious life of her and her daughter on the road as they relocate from one short term academic posting to another. Talbot proves to be a great American chronicler, like the passing moments of life caught by the Leica of beat photographer Robert Frank in *The Americans, The Last Year* elevates fleeting and ephemeral moments, a favourite booth in a bar, a view from a front doorstep, an empty flat left behind, to a profound view of what makes us who we are.

— Felicity Jones, Actress and Producer

# THE LAST YEAR

## ESSAYS

Jill Talbot

JILL TALBOT

For Sarah -
Here's to the last year
and to strength it takes
to let go.
Jill
August 2023

Wandering Aengus Press
wanderingaenguspress.com

First Edition. Published by Wandering Aengus Press

Nonfiction
ISBN: 979-8-218-13930-8
Author Photo: Cicily Bennion
Cover Photo: Clifton Weins
Book Design: Jill McCabe Johnson

"Road Grad" was originally published in *Longreads*. Versions of all the other essays originally appeared in *The Paris Review Daily* as a column, "The Last Year."

Wandering Aengus Press is dedicated to publishing works to enrich lives and make the world a better place.

Wandering Aengus Press
PO Box 334 Eastsound, WA 98245
wanderingaenguspress.com

# Table of Contents

For Indie

# Prologue

# Road Grad

The showers had been steady for days. Even when the rain broke, the weather app on my phone showed another coming storm. At night, lightning scarred the sky, jagged answers to the crack of thunderous questions. A relentless deluge, like so much else last year.

☙

In the spring of 2020, the bottom corner of TV screens broadcasting news channels recorded the rising numbers of deaths and cases, along with Dow numbers shifting, sometimes in seconds, from green to red.

During the spring break of my daughter Indie's senior year, her school district announced they would close schools the week following the break, with plans to reopen on March 23. On March 19, the governor of Texas temporarily closed schools until April 3, then later extended the order to May 4, and on April 17, he closed all private and public schools for the remainder of the year, while initiating steps to re-open the state for business. Indie would finish her senior year in her bedroom. She would not step back through the front doors of her high school, and she would not place her hands in purple ink and press them to a wall or write her name and 2020 beneath her handprints. There would be no Bronco Walk, when seniors paraded the school halls behind the drum corps in their caps and gowns as teachers and students came out of classrooms to cheer, while parents lined the main lobby boasting signs of celebration and congratulations. I would have cried, I am sure, standing there, holding a sign for Indie.

During those first weeks at home, Indie told me more than once how she wished she had known that the last day she left school was the last time. She grew up with so many goodbyes, so she knows the importance of looking back in those moments before leaving.

Up until that week in March, as Indie left for school each morning, I'd stand beneath the canopy of an oak tree outside to watch her go. She'd always look back as she pulled away, and I'd blow kisses and wave my arms wildly. I mourned those mornings. They ended before I knew they were gone.

I raised Indie on my own.

After her father left, disappearing one July morning when she was four months old, I understood the most important thing I would do in my life was raise Indie. When she was two, I promised myself not to date until she was grown. I worried about men coming and going through her life, but more importantly, I recognized my responsibility, and while I have a history of being irresponsible in my life, I wanted to get this one right. The promise kept.

Through the years, I went to every parent-teacher conference alone. I taught Indie how to ride her bike. How to drive a car. How to dive into a pool. I watched her write her first word, *apple*. Heard her first word, *juice*. I decided punishments, and I chose rewards. For every birthday, I woke her by walking into her room with a lit candle in a pastry and singing "Happy Birthday." On the days when daycare was closed or I couldn't afford it, I took her to my office or into my classrooms. I explained to every pediatrician and one ER doctor that no, I don't know the father's medical history. I shook hands with the boys who picked her up for dates, set her curfew at 11:30, the same one I had had in high school in the eighties. Then that morning three years ago, when I had to tell her that her grandfather was suddenly gone, and two months later, when I waited for her to get home to say the words, "Gramma has cancer. Stage IV." I taught my daughter how important it is to apologize, and I told her, "I'm sorry," every time I made a mistake or yelled or we had to move, again, because for 11 years, the academic job market awarded me only visiting positions. The first time we moved, from Colorado to Utah, Indie was 16 months old, and by the time she entered eighth grade in Texas, we had lived in nine states.

And because of that, we are most who we are when we're on the road.

As the weeks went by, I worked at our kitchen table teaching my creative writing workshops on my laptop, while Indie studied on her bed in her room. Around six each night, we'd meet on the couch to watch our shows and visit, often agreeing how lucky we were that we get along so well, that we enjoy each other's company. Because that's what we were for months, each other's company.

We stayed up late, and we slept late. For the five years we'd lived in this apartment, I'd hear the wail of trains in the middle of the night, and in the mornings, the roar of planes in their descent to the DFW airport, twenty-five miles south. That spring, no train whistles called out in the night, and the morning skies were empty.

After a while, I could sense a looming sadness and restlessness in both of us, so one night I asked Indie if she wanted to go the next day to see what the World's Largest Casino looked like closed. Her face lit up. The next morning, we drove forty-five miles north, crossed the Oklahoma border, and took Exit 1 to WinStar. We drove slowly around the sprawling property the size of a community college campus, if one were to have a three-tower hotel and 600,000 square feet of gaming centers. No cars or people in sight, except for a security guard patrolling on a bike. I rolled down my window and snapped a few photos of the desolation, an eerie site. On the way back, we saw an abandoned one-story motel and pulled over to wander among the empty, exposed rooms, and the diamond-shaped windows, most of them broken. That out-and-back drive would turn out to be our first half-tank trip.

After that, every two weeks I'd pick a place for us to go, somewhere a half-tank of gas away. Far enough to get away, but close enough not to have to use a gas station restroom. Only after we were in the car would I tell Indie where we were heading — a hotel on a corner square where Frank Sinatra once stayed and Bonnie and Clyde had been spotted, a vacant Futuro House (orange, shaped like a spaceship), a drive-in theater, an empty hotel featured on *Ghost Adventures*, and once, an abandoned post office with a collapsing porch. Along the way, we'd reminisce about all the places we'd lived, as if touring unknown towns reminded us of all the towns we'd known. Or maybe it was facing the ending to the 18 years we shared, so we wanted to remember those places and houses and rooms, to honor them as we passed mile markers and took exits along with Fleetwood Mac's *Greatest Hits.*

cs

The forecast for that Friday read like all the other days before that week. Rain chances at one hundred percent for 7:00 p.m., the hour of Indie's graduation. Instead of the traditional ceremony inside the coliseum of the university where I teach, graduation would be held at the Texas Motor Speedway in Fort Worth, where parents and families would park on the infield to watch graduates cross the checkered finish line on a big screen. The world's largest at 218 feet wide and 94.6 feet tall — 21 stories.

Indie wanted a white dress for graduation, and even though Texas reopened on May 1, I told her I preferred she order a few online. We'd return the ones she didn't choose. I think I'll always see it in my memory, the afternoon she stepped out of her room in a dress rehearsal. A sleeveless, above-the-knee dress, falling in folds between the panels of her purple gown. Cap on. And because the instructions for the ceremony advised against heels because of the long procession around the track, she decided on her white platform Vans.

Over the previous few months, Indie and her friends had had to accept everything that was gone — classes and crowded hallways, prom, playoffs, end-of-the-year concerts, award ceremonies and banquets, yearbook signings, the senior walk, the senior breakfast. The senior walk was the only one that didn't hold any meaning for Indie, a day when DHS seniors put on their caps and gowns to walk the block to the elementary school to thank their first teachers. If Indie were to walk to the elementary schools she attended, she'd have to head north to Oklahoma, on to New York, and back south to Ray Elementary in Chicago. 3,412 miles. Miles she and I drove together over the years, one road after another.

While Indie got ready that Friday, I ironed her dress. I took my time, and every now and again secretly checked the rain chances on my phone. At 4:00, eighty percent. Students were to arrive at the Speedway by 5:30 to have their temperature checked, to answer questions, and to turn in their signed health waiver. If it rained, graduation would not be rescheduled. It would be canceled. I stood there ironing, wanting to ask, "What if it rains?" but I held the question in my throat, knowing Indie already carried it and that she was pushing it to the far back of a drawer of the year's losses.

The first school event of Indie's I attended was when she was in first grade at Will Rogers Elementary. It was a morning assembly, each class from K-3rd performing. When I got out of my car and started walking to the school's office to sign in, I remember whispering, "I'm coming, Indie. I'm here. I'm coming." Inside, I joined other parents leaning against the walls of the gymnasium/auditorium. The students, cross-legged and squirming, sat in rows on the tile floor. When Indie got to her spot on the stage, her blonde hair a bob, wearing a sweet dress my mother had mailed, she began searching for me. I raised my right arm and held my hand as high as it would go. I stretched out my fingers and held them still. I thought my motionless hand might be easier to see among all the waving ones. "It was," she told me when I picked her up from school that afternoon. I told her it was also a secret message —*you are strong, you are steady, I am here.*

Through the years, in the stands of volleyball and basketball games, the auditoriums of plays and choir concerts, the stadiums of band half-time shows and contests, I have sat alone and raised my hand high for Indie, still and steady, even when I knew she couldn't see me because the auditorium lights had already lowered, or I was too far away in the stands.

A few days before graduation, Indie picked up her car passes in a drive-through procession at school, the same way she had returned her textbooks, picked up her yearbook, and turned in her drum major uniform. Each senior was given only two passes — a Student Pass and a Parent Pass. One car for each student, one car for each family.

By 6:00 that night, a reprieve. Blue sky. I got in the car I had been driving for eleven years, one my parents had given me. I headed toward I-35 West for the twenty-mile drive, my Parent Pass on the passenger seat:

VILLAGE OF CHAMPIONS

at Texas Motor Speedway Parent Pass

Class of 2020 Graduation Ceremony

Present this pass for entry into the infield of

TEXAS MOTOR SPEEDWAY

As I joined the line of cars into the Speedway's massive parking lot, I whispered, "I'm coming, Indie. I'm here. I'm coming." I know she can't hear me when I do this, but it always feels like she does. I showed my pass to an attendant, drove through the south tunnel, and followed the directions from orange vests to turn into a gravel space between two pylons.

As the massive screen directed, I tuned my FM radio to 97.7. All around me, the families of 459 graduates. As we waited for the ceremony to begin, the screen featured the graduation photos and activities of each senior. Suddenly, there was Indie, her long blonde hair, her smile, and her accomplishments, including the name of the university in New York she had chosen. I clicked a photo with my phone.

The following Monday, NBC's *TODAY* show would feature the Speedway graduation, showing a long line of seniors in purple DHS masks as "Pomp and Circumstance" played, the rows of white chairs on the track placed six feet apart, and a parking lot of vehicles on the infield facing the 22,000-square-foot screen, honking in celebration.

Imagine the largest drive-in theater in the world — that's what the Speedway became that Friday night, the temperature ninety degrees — a 1,500-acre facility, hundreds of trucks, SUVs, and cars lined up inside an oval track of 1.5 miles ending in a checkered finish line.

What a fitting end — to watch Indie cross a finish line on a road after all the roads we've known. Sitting in my car by myself, ever at the wheel, felt like an honor I had earned by raising her alone.

The students were allowed to remove their masks only as they crossed the checkered line where the superintendent, wearing a mask and gloves, shook their hands and gave them their diplomas. As each graduate crossed, some bowed, some gave a thumbs up, some did a funny dance. I wondered what Indie might do.

As the T names approached, I shifted in my seat, looking for blonde hair, a pink stole, a white dress, Vans. When I heard Indie's name, the first time I had ever heard her full name announced in public, I pressed on my horn and held it, shouting, "Indie! Indie!" She accepted her diploma with a nod, then turned to the camera with a big smile and a wave. Full of joy.

If memory proves anything, it's that we always miss something. Either we can't call up a detail or someone tells us what we didn't see. I suspect there are times when we take in the meaning of the moment more than the details of the moment itself.

Because later that night, when Indie rushed through the front door, still in her gown, she asked, "Did you see it?" She plopped down next to me on the couch, scrolling through her phone. "I figured out a few days ago what I wanted to do. Hold on, someone took a picture of me and got it."

I stared at the photo of my daughter crossing the finish line, beaming, mid-stride.

"I couldn't see you," she explained, "but I knew you could see me."

And then I saw it.

Her right hand held high.

Still and steady.

# Fall

# All Our Leavings

It's late October, and the leaves of the tree outside the door to our apartment in Texas cling to their branches, green and full. Late last night, a surprise rain. Indie and I rushed out to the deluge in bare feet, our T-shirts darkening with each drop. We raised our arms, spinning on the walkway and laughing until lightning seared the sky. I pointed to the tree's thick arms, thinking about the way they stretch as if waving. We huddled under the light on the porch while rivers swelled against the curbs of the parking lot. When I told her we've been running into the rain since she was little, she grinned and nodded, her long blonde hair matted on her shoulders and against her neck. Lately, every moment like this trembles with one idea: our last year.

It has rained less than five inches since July, not a drop in September. We need this release. We are weary from the stubborn heat. But more than that, we are weary from staying here for so long.

Indie was born in Colorado in 2002, in February, when snow shawled the trees. By July, her father was gone, slipped out the door on a Saturday morning before she stirred. I could not know then that she and I would never see him again, the same way I couldn't know our lives, mine and hers, would become a collection of long roads, moving boxes, and change-of-address cards.

When Indie was sixteen months old, I drove us west into Utah to teach writing at a small university. We lived in a corner house with the largest tree in town, a tree with leaves that covered our yard in brown husks the three falls we were there. Those winters, I'd stare out the window, the shadows of the branches like pencil scribbles across the snow. It was there I decided I would not date until Indie was grown. So it has gone all these years, just the two of us.

It was there in Utah, when Indie was two and three and four, that I started the tradition: as soon as we hear rain, we throw open the door. During those first rains, I carried her. She was too young to know my sorrow, the way I waited for word from her father, the way I worried about my bank account every month. But when the rain came, all want and worry washed away. And then in the later rains, she beat me to the middle of the yard or the sidewalk or the walkway.

We left Utah. Then we left Idaho, where a tree outside our duplex spilled yellow-orange onto my windshield. We left Kansas, a room we borrowed, a futon we shared, a tree with branches stretching across a corner of the yard. Then Oklahoma, a tree outside our duplex the setting for the picture I took of Indie in the black-and-white dress she wore on her first day of kindergarten, the morning I told my feet to walk out of Mrs. Brown's room and leave Indie, let Indie, be. Then New York, where a tall tree outside Indie's bedroom window turned the grass into a yellow blanket, and she pushed her scooter through the halls of the English building on the weekends. Then Chicago, where our landlady would give me forty dollars a month to feed the birds that flitted in and out of the tree in her front yard, flutters Indie and I watched from our basement window while we binge-watched *The Office* for the first time. Then New Mexico, and the tree that grew through a hole in the back deck of our adobe home where we liked to sit and watch the headlights curve the mountain, and my father called to tell us every time *Titanic* was showing on TNT. And now Texas, where we've been for five years, the longest we've lived anywhere, where I had the chance to leave a few years ago but didn't because my parents were fifty miles away in the house where I grew up. Now there's a tree at the cemetery, a tree I stare at while I tell the headstone my parents share about Indie, about me. At every leaving, I say to the wind, "I know you know this all already." Then I tell my feet to move.

I don't know trees, how to name them. The same way I may never know how to explain all our leavings. In February, Indie will turn eighteen, and right now, she's sending out her SAT and ACT scores. I know I am not the first person to stand here, but it's the first and only time I will stand here, and I'm standing here now.

This morning, the sun crests the building across the parking lot. I'm waiting under the tree, where last night's rain clings to the leaves like lighted candles. Every school morning, when Indie pulls away in her car, I blow kisses and wave my arms wildly. This morning, an elderly neighbor who's been here longer than we have calls from her balcony. "Soon," she says, her voice like a falling leaf, "I will miss your waving arms."

# Senior Night

The stands at Bronco Field fill early tonight, and the countdown on the scoreboard clocks less than thirty minutes to kick off. On the far end of the field, the Broncos, white jerseys and purple numbers, run defense routes, while green jerseys line up secondary pass plays near the end zone. Four students in purple shirts stand at the edge of the field, each holding a poster-board above their head: FOOTBALL FILLIES CHEER BAND.

We're told to line up alphabetically with our children, so I make my way to the back of the band line. Two cheerleaders and several of the Fillies, in their fringed, drill-team uniforms with hats tied tight, are wearing sashes—SENIOR 2020—and small tiaras.

The couple behind me introduces themselves as Chris Wilson's parents. Chris is one of the sousaphone players. I nod, "Oh, yes, of course," because I remember hearing about the boy who, as a freshman, had to sit on phone books during band practice. When Chris's father asks what instrument my "son? daughter?" plays, I say, "My daughter, Indie. She's the drum major."

I grew up on football fields. My father was the head coach at several high schools in Texas. I like to say I lived *Friday Night Lights* long before the book, the movie, the show. The first games I remember were at Lubbock High in the mid-seventies, the years I was six, seven, and eight. On Saturdays, Dad took me to the field house, where I'd either play school at the chalkboard in the sweaty stench of the locker room or wander the track to a row of bars and practice the pullovers I was learning in gymnastics. On Friday nights in fall, my mother and I huddled under a blanket at the top of the stands, and I'd do a two-footed hop down every step to the concession stand for hot chocolate and a Butternut candy bar.

My father stopped coaching, after thirty-five years, stepping into an administrative role, but he never stopped watching games from his chair in the living room—the college rivalries, the Dallas Cowboys. My mother on the couch, watching with him. As a child, I did, too.

When Indie and I visited my parents, we'd join them to watch the games, and at home, she and I always watched the Saturday games of the university where I was teaching. We once lived a block away from the stadium at Oklahoma State University, where Indie (then seven, eight, or nine) and I sold parking spaces to fans before going inside our duplex to watch the game, highlighted by the roar of the crowd and the brass of the band in the stadium.

In my father's new administrative role, one as purchasing director for the school district, he often visited the large, concrete stadiums in town during games and other events because concession stands were on the long list of his responsibilities. When Indie was old enough, my parents started taking her to the University Interscholastic League marching band contests hosted by the school district, and Indie loved all the bright colors, the music, the formations the band members made on the field. When she started junior high in Texas, Indie picked up the trombone, and in high school, as the only girl in her section, she became its leader. During her sophomore year, the band director encouraged her to try out for one of the drum major positions.

In January of 2017, my father had a heart attack in a hotel room and was gone before my mother could dial 911. Two months later, she was diagnosed with stage IV ovarian cancer, and in the dark of an April morning the next year, while Indie held one of her hands and I held the other, my mother, too, left us.

In early April of her sophomore year, Indie was scheduled to interview for a drum major interview with the band director. Days before, in the hospital, my mother asked me when Indie would find out if she had been selected for drum major. I texted Indie, and she texted back: April 10. When I told my mother the date, she repeated it. And in her voice, the truth: she would not be able to hold on that long.

On the Friday before the funeral, I took Indie to buy clothes for the interview, using my mother's debit card. "Gramma would want to buy you a nice outfit," I told Indie in the dressing room as she turned before the mirror in bare feet, wearing a floral top, a black blazer, and what my mother would have called "a nice pair of black slacks."

That Monday morning, Indie went to the interview, and in a surprise to everyone, including me, she withdrew herself from consideration. The loss of her grandmother, so soon after the loss of her grandfather, she told the band director, was the reason for her withdrawal. She assured him that she would continue as section leader for her junior year and pursue one of the three drum major positions for her senior year. The next year, when she was chosen, along with two young men to be the band's leaders, Indie was selected as the head drum major.

The clock's winding down, and the band parents take turns stepping to the fence to see if the band is heading this way. No, each nods before stepping back into line.

Last week at the Friday morning pep rally, Indie stood in the middle of the gym floor, arm in arm with her best friend, Donte. The two of them were finalists for Homecoming King and Queen. I sat next to Donte's mother in the thundering bleachers, the students in the overcrowded gym stomping a drumroll in the seconds before the big announcement. That night during the game, Indie stood on the podium conducting the band, her HOMECOMING QUEEN sash draped across her crisp uniform, the tiara catching the stadium lights.

Someone in the football line points to the pinks and yellows of dusk, says how lucky we are it's not raining this year. I think about how many parents have stood here, how some of these parents walked with their parents onto this field. Indie and I have been here for five years, a promise I made to her when she entered high school that we wouldn't move again before she graduated.

The game clock closes in on ten minutes, and I hear the rata-tat-tat of the drums, see the first gray uniforms and purple plumes march down Fillmore Street from the band hall, a tradition. I straighten my black blazer and pull at the cuffs of my jeans, question my choice to wear red heels after hearing we'll be walking from the end zone to the fifty.

I was a cheerleader in high school, even college. I used to flip up and down fields like this one.

When I see Indie making her way to me, I glance at the top of the stands and imagine my mother there, a blanket across her lap, clapping. I look to the sidelines, remember my father pacing, pacing. And I remember all the running starts I took on the field before flipping, flipping, flipping. Indie rushes up and takes her place in line, and I look up at her, the way I've had to do for years, even in heels. Chris Wilson slides in behind us, taller than both of his parents. Indie's friends cross the field, arm in arm with one parent on one side, one on the other. Donte's parents, divorced for over a decade, walk together with their son.

At the edge of the field, the band director speaks names into a small mic, a direct line to the press box. We step up beside him. Indie's wearing her white gloves. She grabs my hand and squeezes. The band director presses a button and whispers: "Talbot, ready to go."

# We Lived Here

I've never owned a house or a refrigerator, never had to think about knobs for cabinets. The cabinets in our apartment don't have knobs, and it's not for the sake of sleekness or simplicity. It's cheap, functional. Lately, every time I open the front door, I wonder how many strangers have closed it for the last time. I wonder what might have caused the painted-over dents on the wall in my bathroom. And I wonder if someone else stared at the gap between the front door and the foundation the way I do, saw the sunlight sneak through during the day, felt the cold scuttle in across the floor at night.

Every time Indie and I have moved, I've rented a place sight unseen, because I can't afford to make the trip to the new town to scout rentals, walk room to room, peek in closets. I'm easily swayed: I said yes to the house in Utah when the landlady on the phone said, "It's on a corner"; yes to the duplex in Oklahoma because a Craigslist photo showed a built-in bookshelf in the living room; and yes to this apartment complex because the website showed black appliances, and we'd never had black appliances before.

Last year, I decided to rent a house. I wanted to give Indie two things for her last year at home: one, a place to practice trombone without worrying about the neighbors, and two, her own bathroom, which she's never had.

Not long before my mother died, she worried about my inability to make decisions. She told me it had been her fault, hers and my father's, that they had made all my choices for me when I was growing up. I suppose that's true.

When I went to the apartment office to put in our sixty-day notice, I asked the receptionist, "What happens if I change my mind?" She assured me that as long as I came back in before the lease was up in May, I could sign a new one.

Indie started zooming through Zillow and Trulia, lugging her laptop onto the couch every night, showing me gray-carpet living rooms and backyards, asking the budget, X-ing out ones that exceeded it. We drove down tree-lined streets for walk-throughs, but the rooms either reminded us (in a bad way) of a place we had lived before, or I'd call the number on the sign out front to hear it had been rented that morning. The weeks went by.

Indie and I contextualize our lives, the years, by cities: "We were in Canton, so you were nine, ten"; "That last year in Stillwater, so it would have been 2011"; or "You remember a mirror on the back of the bathroom door? Cedar City." We can pack boxes and run tape across them and keep track of the Sharpie pen through the span of a few viewings of *Tootsie*, our moving movie. The one that plays while we pack and fill garbage bags, the kind of bags meant for leaves.

When we had only a week left in our lease, I went to tell the apartment manager we'd be staying. He pulled out a black binder, flipped to a spreadsheet, told me our apartment had been rented. The receptionist, it turns out, had been let go weeks before, and someone was scheduled to move into our home, our rooms, our kitchen, our bathroom, in eleven days.

Indie and I have a tradition: on our last day living somewhere, after a truck has backed up and hauled away the moving pod, when the rooms are empty and the shower curtainless, we leave pennies. I give Indie a few, grab some for myself, and we disappear into our own spaces, leaving a penny on a windowsill or on the floor where my writing desk had been or on a shelf in her room. We only tell each other where we placed them, and why, after we've gone.

When the apartment manager offered us a two-bed, two-bath apartment across the parking lot for the same rent, I went out to the storage closet on the patio and started pulling out empty boxes, the same ones we've always used for all our moves. Cue *Tootsie*. Sharpie on the kitchen counter, packing tape, a box of black bags. We kept thinking how we had lived in this apartment longer than we had lived anywhere. With every pull of tape, every BOOKS written on a box, every time Indie dragged a bag from her room across the floor, I thought, *This is the last time we'll move together*. The next move will be hers alone.

This complex has signals for vacant apartments: blinds closed and the dining room light on means *this one needs maintenance or cleaning*. Blinds open means *the apartment's ready*. The doors, I discovered years ago, remain unlocked until move-in day. On the last night before the new tenants were scheduled to arrive in June, I hurried across the parking lot with a blue Bic pen and slowly opened the door to our old apartment, the light from the streetlamp crossing the dark floor in lines. Here was where Indie played her trombone, where I wrote essay after essay, where I stood in her doorway to tell her that her grandfather was gone and where we returned that morning after my mother passed, where Indie posed for a picture in a blue dress for prom, and where I shook the hand of her first date. I opened the front closet, stepped inside, and wrote on the inside wall: "We lived here. 2015-2019."

Sometimes I use Google Maps to look at the places we've lived, to see how they've changed. It's strange to live across from our old apartment, to look through the blinds to see strangers moving through rooms we knew. This morning, when I stood outside to wave as Indie pulled away for school, I noticed the two garden hooks she had screwed in on either side of our balcony for hanging baskets. Empty.

# A Corner Booth

I'm sliding into the corner booth when Steve sets down a water with two limes, the napkin already damp. About once a week, I drive two towns over—twenty minutes along the backroads beyond I-35—to write here. I call it my Writing Restaurant, and the only person who knows it's *this* restaurant is Indie. I text her before I take off, let her know where I'm headed. I'll stay here for most of the day.

A year ago, Indie got her first job here as a host, so I stopped coming to let her have this space for herself, but now she works at another restaurant a few miles from where we live.

I'm glad to have my booth back.

I like the drive, the disappearing, the secret. No one knows that while I'm sitting in this booth, I'm pulling into a gravel drive in Colorado or stepping off a bus on Michigan Avenue or playing Uno with Indie in a restaurant miles and states and years from here.

When Indie was about three, she woke in the middle of the night unable to sleep. I turned on the kitchen light, and she and I sat on the floor eating cherry sours and talking until we were sleepy enough to wander back to our beds. It felt like a secret world. That night, I realized that as a single parent, I could let Indie eat cherry sours in the middle of the night if I wanted to. I was the only one around to say *yes* or *no* or—as she's gotten older and the questions have become more difficult—*Let me think about it.*

That night, the joy of those cherry sours: simple.

We lived in southern Utah then, and on Thursday nights, we'd go eat at Main Street Grill where a fifty-something man named Jack, always in creased jeans and cowboy boots, a starched Western shirt, sang country into a microphone in the corner. Jack managed the State Liquor Store across the street and dyed his hair a different shade of blonde every few weeks. Indie and I'd sit down in a booth just as Jack was plugging in his speaker, doing a mic check. He'd wave, wink. His set list was a rotation of Conway Twitty, George Jones, the slow Cash songs. His voice was a rough whisper over the clinks of forks against plates, and when he got to any line with "loving you" in it, he'd aim his eyes on me. Indie, perched on her knees and peeking over the top of the booth to see Jack, always giggled when he did that. Jack kept his distance. There was a world of sadness in him, but I had my own, still hoping back then that Indie's father would come home.

Not long after Indie was born, I found a receipt in his wallet. Dinner and drinks for two. I woke him up in the night. He didn't even try to talk his way out of it. Just made me feel like I was the one who'd done something wrong.

From across the restaurant, Steve gives me a thumbs up. I give one back and nod. I like that the servers here leave me alone.

I think it must have started with tic-tac-toe, when Indie and I played on napkins or kid menus. Once, when we were in Chili's marking Xs and Os, an elderly woman and her husband shuffled by our table on their way out. The woman leaned over and put her hand on my shoulder, "You're a good mother." I smiled and thanked her but wondered if what she said was true. Still do.

Indie and I have always enjoyed each other's company, and just the other day, she told me a friend asked how I knew about something. She told him what she tells everyone, "My mother and I talk about everything." That I know to be true, but it's also part of the worry. The worry that I've asked more of her, at times, than I should, to be a confidant rather than just a child. The worry that I haven't sheltered her as much as I've shown her the seams.

When we eat out, usually at the beginning of the month, we like to go early, 4:30, 5:00, when the place is mostly empty. We settle in and set up. For years it was Connect Four. Two of us at a high top in Eskimo Joe's in Stillwater, Oklahoma, taking turns dropping red and black checkers down the slots, the pieces spilling from the bottom onto the table for another game. We've shuffled cards for Go Fish, Hearts, and Uno, more than any other. At Buffalo Wild Wings, we'd each get a game console and play Buzztime trivia, or I'd give her a roll of quarters for the Claw Game. Just the other day, she told me how much she loved those days at B-Dubs, quarter after quarter. I confessed that those were the times I needed a minute. That was the secret of the Claw Game.

Looking back—on Jack and trivia and all our games—I see it all as my way of letting Indie leave the world behind, the world she's always been so keenly aware of. But a few months ago, I took the Uno cards out of my glove box. I don't remember when we stopped playing, but I remember it was in this booth, when Indie started a story about some friends at school and the choices they were making, choices that carried them away from her, the same choices I warned her against when she entered high school. She no longer needed, I understood, to let the world fall away, because she's finding her own world, and she needs my help understanding it. She needs to ask difficult questions, the kind I often answer with stories from when I was her age.

We still have an Uno deck in the glove compartment of my car, and the Connect Four game we keep in a trunk in the living room. The last time we played Uno was at this very booth a few months ago, and I remember Indie pulling the deck from the glove compartment then dropping it in the parking lot, all the cards daring to flutter away in the wind. I thought then it was a sign of something ending. When we play games now, we play at home—Scrabble or a puzzle in progress on a card table.

We meet at restaurants these days, when we both finish with school or she gets off work, and with her band and work and friends, and I take myself out to eat alone more and more. Sometimes I take my laptop and write. Sometimes I just sit in the nearly empty restaurant and take a minute.

# GHOSTS

My mother bought the kitchen table in 1969. It's dark maple, four chairs, their backs a row of five slats. The etchings of my math homework mark the wood, but the busiest scratches cover the space between my parents' seats, like the ghosts of all they passed across the table and what they must have said. My mother always sat across from me, my father to my left, and eventually Indie sat across from my father. When he died, my mother sat in her chair at the table calling friends, one by one, to tell them he was gone. I don't remember eating at the table after that. On the morning after my mother's funeral a little over a year later, I sat in my chair at the table writing checks, paying her bills, signing her name.

In January, Indie and I left my parents' house for the last time. A house built when I was nine, in 1979. I remember walking through it when it was only a concrete slab and a fireplace. That afternoon, as I moved to stand in the door of each room, I kept saying *thank you* as if my parents were there, as if they could hear me. All the furniture and the décor still intact, the way I wanted to remember the house. Indie and I packed up my childhood bedroom suite, my father's chair, his cherrywood stereo console, boxes of my mother's belongings, her two white suitcases (a high school graduation present from 1963), and the kitchen table. Left the rest for the estate sale. When I closed the back door for the last time, I was forty-nine. Indie considered it her childhood home too, the only one that had been consistent throughout her life. She was sixteen.

Yesterday, for the first time since we had moved the kitchen table into our apartment, she and I sat down to eat at it. It had taken us ten months. Indie stood with a hand on the back of her chair and asked, "How do the seats work here?" I set down the placemats: "We sit where we always sat."

When we moved to Stillwater, Oklahoma, Indie was five. Back then, her bright blonde bob was always tousled. She had her own room in the duplex I rented, but she never slept in it. For four years, she slept close to me on the futon a friend had given us on his way out of town. The day I signed the lease on the hood of the manager's truck, she looked over at the front door and muttered something about the past tenants, a brick through the front window. Later, Indie picked up half a brick in the yard, and for as long as we lived there, we'd find the glass, piece after piece.

It was in Oklahoma when Indie first told me about the ghosts. She made me promise I wouldn't write about them. And I never have. Until now.

At the kitchen table, we started reminiscing—something we've started doing more and more during this last year, a way to recognize and name what's built or broken our lives. This time we talked about the ghosts, the ones in Oklahoma, New York, New Mexico, even here in Texas. When I reminded her that she had asked me not to write about them when she was little, she said, "You can write about them now."

In New Mexico, when Indie was twelve, we lived in an adobe house, the oldest house in town. We were sitting in her room one night when she heard footsteps outside the door, steps across the back deck. I didn't hear them, but I ran to the kitchen and called the police while Indie peeked through the window to see a shadow on the deck. The police didn't find anyone around the house, but we never heard the steps of anyone leaving, a sound neither one of us would have missed.

I'm not writing about all the ghosts here.

Indie described them as strangers, men who shuffled around in dark suits, women in dresses who'd come stand next to her, all kind, friendly, smiling. Sometimes kids. It was the little girl and her dog standing in the corner of Indie's room in the duplex who terrified her. The one that showed up often, looking like she needed help. After that, Indie kept her door closed most of the time. I didn't like going in there, either.

Once in Oklahoma, I sat in the stands watching Indie at swim lessons, when she suddenly draped her arm over the edge of the pool and looked up into the stands, smiling. Not at me, but somewhere farther down the bench. While I drove us home, she told me it was a good day, and when I asked why, she said, "Because Great-Grandma was in the stands, watching me swim." My father's mother, the woman who once showed us how to make her chocolate pie, a secret recipe.

For forty years, I moved through the rooms of a house where others move now. I still have the key to that house on my keychain, as if I could step up to the front door at any time and unlock it, walk into the living room, and turn on the lamp.

After my parents were gone, Indie and I often made the hour drive to their house on weekends to feel close to them, to water my mother's flowers, to make it look like someone still lived there. But most of the time, the house was empty, so I bought an alarm system, one I kept on until the day the new owners were given the keys and moved in. The night before they did, I checked the activity log on the app and found a long list of detected movements in the living room, my parents' room, out the back patio door, into the garage, back and forth, over and over again. As if they were there. But the house, I knew, was empty.

I put my father's stereo console in my room, and when I'm in there, sitting at my desk or turning back my bed, I hear something inside the stereo, a boom, tubes from a system manufactured in the seventies. All those decades my father kept his Johnny Cash and Jerry Lee Lewis records spinning, I never once heard it. Now when the console pops in my room, I ask, "What is it, Daddy?"

One night in New York, when Indie was nine, maybe ten, we were sitting on the couch in the house we rented, a house Indie said was "crowded" the day we moved in. She turned suddenly, as if she had been called by someone. I turned, too. "There, in the doorframe," she said, staring.

When Indie or I make my grandmother's chocolate pie, we always linger on the first bite. It all comes back to us, the twang in her voice, the day she taught us to make it, our missing a little softer in those moments.

The night of my mother's funeral, I slept on top of the comforter on my parents' bed and woke to a figure in the doorway: "Indie, if you're going to stand there, come get in bed with me." Not long after, I heard Indie's voice calling out from the living room where she had been sleeping. She said Gramma had been standing by the foldout couch, watching her.

Yesterday we sat for a long time after the plates were empty, exchanging stories. Indie said people don't follow her anymore, but she does feel energy clinging to her sometimes, and when it gets really strong, like when she's leaving a room, she rushes out and closes the door. I didn't tell her this, but I have noticed how often she closes doors quickly, almost slamming them. I asked if that's why she leaves the light by her bed on all the time, even when she's not there. She laughed, her long blonde hair spilling across her face: "No, I just forget to turn it off!" Our laughter built, broke us free. We got up to put our plates away, and I looked back at the table—two placemats, two empty places—the missing a little softer in that moment.

The ghosts that follow us now are ones we know. This time next year, I'll move through these rooms alone.

# Winter

# Trains

Trains thundered through that town, behind the woods that bordered our backyard. I'd stand at the kitchen sink and watch out the window, catching only flashes of the cars through crowded branches. I envied the train's travel, imagined some town down the line and wondered if I'd been there before. It always felt as if I had. Those trains rumbling through northern New York all passed by midmorning, leaving the afternoon to rest quiet in their absence. I remember snow falling in diagonal lines, the woods silver-gray.

Indie liked to wander those woods behind the house we rented. She would have been ten or eleven then, her blonde hair a bob. She'd take a backpack and a walking stick with her, and I'd open the back door and call after her, remind her to watch the time, the light, and in winter, the snow's depth. She'd turn and wave as the woods drew a curtain behind her. Once she came back to tell me about a pond with beaver dams, and another day she stomped snow from her boots in the breezeway while sharing her discovery: railroad tracks.

Not long after Indie was born, her father began searching online for an old truck. The truck idea was a part of a slow shift, like the guitar he learned to play, the thick beard he grew, the flannel shirts he started ironing before leaving for his maintenance job at a resort, where a woman in the event-planning office paid him just enough attention.

When he found a blue 1978 Chevy C20 Bonanza with a white camper, he caught the Amtrak in Denver and rode it to King Street in Seattle. It took him almost two days to get there, longer to drive back. When he called from the station in Washington, he sounded far away, but not the kind of far I could measure by miles.

During those summer days in Boulder while he was gone, Indie rocked in her swing to Simon and Garfunkel's *Greatest Hits* while I sat on our balcony reading *Door Wide Open*, a collection of letters between Jack Kerouac and Joyce Johnson written from March 1957 to November 1958. While I read, I kept the balcony door open, the screen door shut. From out there, everything appeared in shadow: the futon against the wall, the CD player on top of the TV, the back and forth of the swing, even the calendar on the kitchen wall, the one with trains in black-and-white. I remember staring into the apartment, feeling as if I were looking at a photograph of something that would soon end, and I couldn't do anything to stop it. I knew before I knew, I was already looking back.

While Johnson waited in her Village apartment for Jack to come and go, and Jack dashed off postcards from Mexico City and Orlando and San Francisco, I realized I had my own Kerouac running rails and riding roads to places I still haven't been. And then Indie's father came home one morning long enough to say he was going. It was that sudden. And for the rest of that year, I left the numbered boxes on the calendar blank. I couldn't bear to record any of those days, to name them. Every month I flipped the calendar to find another train before me, still. I'd stare at each one, wonder how time kept moving.

I don't like to write about Indie's father. I've done enough of that. But in this last year together at home, before Indie leaves for college, he is noticeably absent. She and I talk about him now and then. It's as if he's a man we saw once, missing a train. A stranger left behind at the station.

When Indie was eleven, she and I took the Amtrak from Chicago, where we lived that year, to Dallas to visit my parents. Neither of us had been on a train before, and we loved rocking along, stopping at the small brick stations, seeing passengers shuffle on the platform. After twenty stations across four states, I was surprised to realize we were riding the stretch of tracks that ran behind my parents' house, the house I had lived in since I was nine. How mysterious it felt to watch the streets I knew so well from the window of a train. As if I had never been there before.

The other day I found a calendar in a box, "Classic Trains," twelve steam engine locomotives from the year I checked into rehab after wine became a route I took too often. Indie stayed with a very kind family, friends, until I returned during the first days of January and bought the calendar. Many of my fellow patients were railroad workers, men who rode trains in the middle of the night. For months after we all got out, a couple of them would call every other week or so from a train. If there's a sound to the middle of nowhere in the middle of the night, I heard it through the phone. I wish I still had the voice mail from the mustachioed hay-farmer-turned-railroad-worker, the message he left the exact hour (3 a.m.) of Indie's fourth birthday. I remember every word: "Jill, it's your ol' pal, Andy. I'm riding the rails through some field in Oregon, but I'm going to break the rules and sound the four whistles for Indie's birthday. I love ya, Jill." And then the whistles sounded—one after another—as lonesome as I imagine we all can be sometimes. That was the last time I heard Andy's voice. I lost track of him, or we lost track of each other, the way the counselors assured us we all would.

In Texas in the middle of the night, the train whines beyond the woods outside my bedroom window. I turn over, half asleep, and sink into the sound of passing through, of going and gone, the four-whistle warning. Here, about forty miles from Dallas, the trains sing through every hour.

In his first novel, *The Town and the City*, Kerouac writers about Peter Martin, a young man with a desire to go, to leave his hometown for a wider world, hearing "some unspeakably exciting foregathering of events in the woods." Indie often speaks of her own desires to go, to leave. At first, her repeated declarations of readiness and impatience to leave left a lingering sting, but eventually I realized I raised her to know, as Kerouac also wrote, "how easy the act of leaving was, and how good it felt."

Again, *The Town and the City*: "Suddenly there was the rumbling of the train coming ... the giant engine overtopped them passing in a tremendous flare ... It was time, time ... the train ... moving, moving."

This last year with Indie is a thundering train.

The woods of what's to come a curtain.

Listen, there's the train now.

# Turtle, Turtle

Childhood is full of fictions, at least it should be. When Indie was little, her favorite game to play in the pool was Turtle, Turtle. She'd climb on my back, and I'd swim around saying "Turtle, Turtle," the way you'd say "Ribbit, Ribbit" for a frog.

We found him in my parents' backyard pool, all four of his legs flipping. Indie was seven that summer. She and I had been taking one last swim before heading back to Oklahoma, four hours north. While I dove down, Indie stood on the steps of the pool. The turtle, a red-eared slider, was tiny, about the size of my palm. Indie named him Flipper.

We lived in a duplex those four years in Oklahoma. We had a little garden patch beneath our front window. There were four units in all, so we shared a sidewalk with an opera singer who worked at the grocery store, a large, loping Marine who had done two tours in Afghanistan, and a frumpy student who mostly wore brown and sat outside to study in a chair from his kitchen. I had a visiting professor's salary, and there wasn't a month when we made it to the thirtieth or thirty-first before we ran out of money.

Indie and I made a home for Flipper out of a kitty litter box, a blue one. We filled it with rocks, grass, and leaves, and put it in our garden.

He was a happy turtle. He'd bask on one of his rocks in the corner or burrow beneath a layer of leaves. When we'd find him with his right front leg stretched out, we'd know he was sleeping.

For the people in our duplex community, life was either on hold or had no hold. At night, the singer played piano, practiced trills, but sometimes she played another song, long and loud sobs, an opera of despondence. The Marine stared at the blare of his oversize TV from his couch, working through a twelve pack every night, and the student made the same walk to the grocery store every day, a drooping plastic bag in each hand. We wondered what their real stories might be. I'm sure they wondered about mine.

I don't know when I made up the story, but at some point I told Indie that Flipper's house was a coffee shop he ran called Sinatra's. From sunup to sundown, Flipper took orders, whipping up frozen cappuccinos and lattes. He even had a little apron, like the one the Marine wore when he cooked. And the student, on his daily errand, bought the ingredients and supplies Flipper needed. Indie and I'd step out to the porch and order drinks, and we'd marvel at the long line or see that it was a slow day, and some mornings, one of us would guess the muffin from the scent—cinnamon.

Our neighbors liked to say hello to Flipper when they passed, coming and going, but when we told them about Sinatra's, we started hearing them ask things like, "Hey, Flipper! How's business?" or order a vanilla latte.

One day, the opera singer knocked on our patio door and held up a three-inch plastic dinosaur, purple and yellow. She said she thought Flipper could use some help. Indie rushed out and set the dinosaur on top of a rock in the middle of the café. We named him Frank.

That coffee shop gave us all a fiction we needed.

# First Snow

A silver mixing bowl, that's what I remember my mother handing me. I was five. My first snow ice cream. For five years, my daughter and I have lived in this Texas town. For five years, no snow. But this morning, snow rushed down as my daughter slept. I snuck outside and cupped enough from the hood of her car. Milk, vanilla, sugar, and a pinch of salt. My mother's bowl.

This is not missing. This is us, living.

# Pendulum

I grew up inside the smoke of my grandmother's Pall Malls. The air between her and my mother was just as stifling. On our visits to East Texas, the two women would sit in stiff silence for what seemed like hours to my six-year-old sense of time. My mother sat on the brocade couch, my grandmother in her gold velour chair. In every room, there was at least one painting of flowers—roses or daises—all of them done by my grandmother. I'd sit on the floor, counting the chimes from the grandfather clocks in the hallway, not one of which kept the same time as any other. After my grandmother had wandered off to the back room to clink the crystal decanter against her highball glass too many times, we'd go. My mother never left without leaning over that gold chair to kiss her mother goodbye. She never left without saying, "I love you," like a sigh you let out when the night's too long. Then that high-chinned stride for the screen door. Every time, just before my mother pushed it open, my grandmother would surrender: "Love you, Martha Jo."

The day I found out I was having a girl, I sat in my car in the parking lot of the doctor's office and sobbed. Deep, ragged sobs.

A few months after my mother died, I was in her kitchen with Mary and Jean, her two best friends, whom she had known since the first grade. While I pulled down pieces of china from the kitchen hutch and wrapped each one in newspaper, Mary and Jean helped Indie, at sixteen, pack her own set of dishes, the ones my grandmother gave to my parents when they married in 1969. That china set was hand-painted with pink roses, had gilded handles and my grandmother's initials on the bottom of each delicate piece. Mary and Jean's mothers had taken the same painting classes as my grandmother. As Mary liked to say, "What else was there to do in that small town in the fifties?" Mary and Jean still live in that small town.

I placed an empty box on the kitchen table and asked the question I had never been able to ask my own mother: "How bad was my grandmother's drinking?" None of us stopped packing while they took turns telling stories—my grandmother's long drives to the closest wet county, the afternoon she "took a nap" during one of their Girl Scout meetings, an ad she put in the newspaper for her lost red purse with two possible locations where it might have been left.

My mother-grief trembles. Regret, apology, a deep missing. When I sit inside it—as when I pull on one of her sweaters or use her measuring spoons or listen to her Patsy Cline CD—the ache feels like a cacophony of clock chimes. My mother and I never kept the same time.

After all the boxes were taped, Mary and Jean grabbed their purses. I walked them out to the driveway and said I didn't feel like my mother ever really liked me. Mary hugged me close and whispered in my ear, "Jill, she loved you." Jean sighed, "She just never learned how."

Eighteen years ago, with my daughter growing inside me, I knew I contained a difficult history—my mother and her mother, my mother and me. I could feel it ticking, ticking, ticking.

After I left home for college, I often went to East Texas alone to visit my grandmother. As a child, I'd only known the lonely widow who kept cashews on the kitchen counter, the woman who pretended there wasn't bourbon in the back room. I wanted to know more. During those solo visits, she'd tell me stories—about my mother, the man she sent a Dear John letter to during the war, the time she caught my mother and Mary smoking (Mary denies this)—but mostly she'd gossip about the neighbor across the way. Sometimes we'd laugh so hard she'd fall into a fit of Pall Mall coughing.

Indie has the same shoe size as my mother and kept some of her shoes. Her favorite is a pair of black suede bootees with a thick wedge heel. She wears them every time she has a band concert, an audition, something special. Last week, before leaving for a jazz festival, she came home from the store with superglue, said that one of Gramma's heels had come loose.

Most nights, Indie and I like to sit on the couch and watch one of our shows. She puts her feet in my lap, and every few minutes, we hit pause to tell each other a story from our day or update an ongoing saga: "Okay, do you remember when I told you?" One-hour shows take us two hours to finish. We like to stretch the time.

I never knew how much Indie and my mother talked and texted until Indie opened a present, one of the last ones, it turned out, that my mother gave her. It was a floral duvet cover, black with gray and rose-pink flowers. "We picked it out together," Indie told me. Sometimes when I'm in Indie's room, I smooth the flowers on the bed.

In the hospital, when I knew it was time to say what I needed to say to my mother, I held her hand and began, "Thank you," and as I continued, the words that were pushing from the back of my throat—the ones I really wanted to say—wouldn't come out. *I'm sorry.*

When Indie was an infant, I'd sit on the couch with my feet on the coffee table, my knees bent. I'd place Indie on my thighs and take her hands to sing "Do-Re-Mi." I made up hand movements for each note—so that she'd trace sundrops as if they were falling rain for re, tap, tap, tap her own heart for mi, and pump her arms for the long run of fa, her favorite. She doesn't remember it. But I do. I remember it as the first time I knew we would reverse the pendulum's swing.

# The Phone Call

As the first anniversary of my father's death approached, my mother asked me to put roses on his grave: "I want him to have them for the day." She wasn't well enough to do it herself—the cancer had taken its last turn, though we didn't know it then. When she died, fourteen months after my father, I swiped through the photos on her phone and found his grave, its mound of funeral flowers. He was buried on the first of February, and the dates on the photographs showed she had driven the hour there on the second, the third, the fourth, and the fifth. Disbelief, I imagine, and the need to convince herself it was true.

My father died in the hotel room where my parents were staying in McKinney, Texas. A heart attack at eighty-three. He was gone before my mother could get to the phone. He was gone when the paramedics asked him his name. He was gone when the ambulance rushed away, my mother following in their car to the emergency room.

On the second anniversary of my father's death, last year, Indie and I were at my parents' house for the final time, packing boxes, going through drawers and closets, watching movers load the furniture we wanted before the estate sale. The day came and went.

After driving fifty miles on US 380 to McKinney, I take I-75 south toward the Ridgeview exit then take a right toward the cemetery. I follow the winding path to the tree and park beside it. I cross the grass to the headstone, the one my parents share. This is the first anniversary I have had the chance to really remember—the daze of a drive Indie and I made on 380 East that Saturday morning, the corners we turned in the ER until we found my mother in the doorway watching for us, my father's body in the room behind her. I kneel down and press my fingertips to the date: January 28, 2017.

Indie's at work today, so she'll come to the cemetery by herself tomorrow. I will not write her grief here, only mine.

My father would get a paper plate and fill it with Nilla wafers, then grab a knife and spread peanut butter on each one; race popsicle sticks with me in the rush of water along the curb after it rained; play his Jerry Lee Lewis albums loud enough to hear while he was in shower; spin our orange VW Bug in the mall parking lot when it snowed ("Don't tell your mother"); recount the entire plot of the movie he had gone to see by himself; prop his feet on the rubber rails of escalators as we descended, one foot on each side; call me whenever *Titanic* was on TV; follow me to my car every time I left to go back to college to tell me, "Remember why you're there"; write me letters on yellow legal-pad pages; drive me to downtown Dallas and walk the 5K route while I ran; ask the piano player in Nordstrom to play "La Vie en Rose"; order a waffle, *crisp*, bacon, *crisp*; swim laps at dusk while Indie swam beside him.

Every time I visit the cemetery, I talk to my parents. I look at the tree, and I tell them things. But today, after I remove the poinsettias and walk them down to the dumpster, after I set the roses in the vase and arrange them until I can hear my mother saying, "Pretty," I stand silent. I think about next year when Indie will be at college, and how, then, everyone will be gone.

I won't mind being alone. I've always felt most myself when I'm by myself, but still, Indie will go in seven months, and her leaving will be another loss in a litany of losses. All of them, one after another. The soon of Indie's leaving trembles like a last train car.

Across the way, a tractor bounces over the grass to dig a new grave.

Three days from now, on January 28, I will wake while it's still dark, unable to sleep while the rain slows. I'll turn over and back again, throwing back the covers, feeling dread. Later, I will sit with Indie at the kitchen table and tell her, "It's as if I woke up and felt that phone call coming again." And I will glance at the chair where my father always sat when I say, "The body has a memory." Indie will nod, tell me she woke up in a cold sweat.

I will not tell her that after I left the cemetery, I drove to the Holiday Inn and Suites on I-75. Or that I pulled into the parking lot and drove around the four-story building and figured out there's only one entrance to the hotel. Or that I parked, one of a few cars in the lot, and looked in every direction, wondering which one my father took on his last walk. I do not tell her how I stared at the automatic double doors of the entrance.

Instead, I will tell her about the popsicle sticks, the way Dad would count to three before we let them go, the way he ran alongside his stick, shouting, "Come on, my guy! Come on, my guy!" The way I laughed and ran with him.

# SPRING

# The Envelope

Indie has been on a college tour her whole life—riding in her stroller through the snow in Boulder; rolling down a hill outside the English building in Utah; peering from the passenger window while football fans swarm sidewalks toward a blue field in Idaho; sitting under my office desk in Oklahoma, silently passing me notes or drawing pictures; climbing the three stories to my office in northern New York to race her Razor scooter on the shiny hallway floor; spinning in the revolving doors of a building in Chicago as the El barrels overhead; snapping photos of red-tile roofs in New Mexico; thumbing through the books in my office on a Texas campus covered by trees.

Indie was the first student to show up for kindergarten. Her teacher pointed to a ball of clay on a table, and Indie immediately sat down. I slipped out the door but stood just beyond it, watching her play through the window. Days later, she hopped into the car holding something small and misshapen, painted purple and green. "Here," she said, handing it to me, "I made you a bowl."

In first grade, Indie asked if school could be her space. Because it's always been the two of us, I understood it was important for her to have a world she did not have to share, one she could move through alone. How young she was to ask for this, but as the years have disappeared behind us, I recognize it as a claim my daughter has always made for herself. She will do it alone. I agreed not to interfere unless I had reason: a call from a teacher, a pattern of bad grades, missing work.

I kept my distance, allowed Indie her own.

Last November, she attended a visitation day at a university where I once taught. Out of all the places we've lived, this school stands out as her favorite. I let her go alone. From Dallas, two flights—one to Boston, then a nine-passenger plane farther north. If I had climbed in my car and followed, I would have driven 1,660 miles.

When I was in second grade, my teacher sent a note home requesting a meeting with my parents. I handed over the sweaty note to my mother after waiting as long as I could before bedtime. When she read the note to my father, he sat forward in his chair: "I raised my daughter to be sociable and to have a personality." The next day, my mother walked into Nat Williams Elementary alone.

All through elementary school, the notes from Indie's teachers arrived, tucked into bright folders. The phone rang after dinner or during planning periods. Teachers leaned into my car's window after school: "Are you Indie's mother? Do you have a minute?" At the third-grade parent-teacher conference, Mrs. Schaeffer showed me a desk set apart from the rows, a desk suffocatingly near her own. "That," she said, pointing, "is Indie's desk." Indie, it turns out, had inherited my behavior. I inherited my father's response to it.

Every note, every call, every concern from Indie's teachers was about her talking in class. In seventh grade, when the Spanish teacher called to complain about Indie's laughter, I sat for a moment, then asked, "You're calling me because she's laughing?"

Indie submitted applications to five universities, completing every step of the process on her own, including her selection of schools. She checked email first thing every morning. She walked to the mailboxes at our apartment complex every afternoon, and when she got home late from band rehearsal or work, she'd walk through the door, "Did you check the mail today?" She was accepted to four of the five universities. She was holding out for that last one, the only one she really wanted.

In an attempt to distract her, I started adding a simple sentence to the end of all of my texts to her, followed by its emoji.

Here is a train.

Here is a salad.

Here is a door.

Here is a pen.

Here is a taco.

Here is a television.

She loved it, and her friends did, too. When she texted from English class that her best friend had been accepted to his dream school, I replied, "Here is a highway. To Stillwater."

Imagine going to five schools in seven years. Imagine the conversation you know is coming because of the way your mother sits down on the couch, the way she holds herself and her face, the way she begins, "I got an offer from a school—in Utah, Idaho, Oklahoma, New York, Chicago, New Mexico, Texas."

Now imagine after all those states and moves that you get to pick the state, the school, and stay there.

Imagine that wait.

The morning email checks.

The walks to the mailbox.

Two weeks ago, the bells of the apartment office rang as I stepped inside to tell the manager our garbage disposal wouldn't churn. He held up a finger and disappeared into the package closet. When he stepped out, he handed me a stiff, oversize envelope. The date of its arrival, six days before, had been scribbled in the bottom corner in black sharpie. I rushed out, the bell ringing behind me as I snapped a photo of the insignia in the left corner, the university 1,660 miles away. I sent it to Indie. And then I turned the envelope over and read the words on the back:

"Think about how far you've come—And how far you're about to go."

We hide our small sorrows away.

We search for a way to carry them.

Here is a bowl.

# THE RETURN

I'm aiming my camera at a bench on Pearl Street in Boulder, Colorado. The red-brick path is lined with outdoor shops, galleries, and breweries. Boulder Bookstore. The clouds draw their curtain, a gray weight. The Flatirons are weighted, too, diagonal slabs of sandstone towering like three growing spikes on a graph.

Eighteen years ago, I sat on this bench.

I wait for strangers to step out of the frame. They pass or linger in lace-up boots and parkas, jeans and huddled laughter—all intruders, because while I stand on this brick street in winter, it's really a long-ago afternoon in June.

In "Street Haunting," Virginia Woolf asks, "Is the true self this which stands on the pavement in January, or that which bends over the balcony in June? Am I here, or am I there? Or is the true self neither this nor that, neither here nor there, but something so varied and wandering that it is only when we give the rein to its wishes and let it take its way unimpeded that we are indeed ourselves?"

Maybe we go back to places not to ask questions, but to realize we don't have them anymore.

ଓ

That day in June, my father sat next to me on this bench and said something about how it must be hard to leave a place so beautiful. I looked toward the Flatirons: "There's too much sadness here."

I'm back in Boulder because I want to show my daughter, now eighteen, where she was born, where she lived as an infant, where she began. I want to try to explain who I was here.

I think we harbor our longings for places we've left because we miss who we were in them. I've lingered in door frames and driveways, felt the pierce of pulling away from a past self. The hardest part is knowing what I can't take with me. Because after enough miles and enough passed exits, something dissolves, like light in a room when the sun turns down.

I've always thought I realized a place only after I left it. But maybe it's this, the return.

While I wait to take the photograph, my daughter stands beside me. I have told her the bench's story. She steps closer to me as the sky grows darker, the air colder.

ଓ

For one summer in my late twenties, I lived in a small, two-story house on the banks of the Eagle River in Colorado. A friend coaxed me there, told me she and her husband needed help with the resort-town rent. I settled into their corner room upstairs. One afternoon, not long after I'd arrived, I pulled into the gravel drive and stepped out—I can still hear the crunch of tires against the stones—toward a very tall, bearded man. The fourth roommate. Later, he told me it felt like he had been standing there waiting for me to come home. The summer unfolded. I waited tables at a bar in Vail, and he wired condominiums in the valley.

Seasons come and go, and that summer ended with a phone call from a university offering me a job. I delayed my departure until late August, when the bearded man and I lingered in the gravel drive. He snapped a photograph—my head thrown back in laughter. After I drove thirty minutes down the mountain, I realized I had forgotten my makeup bag. I turned back and found him standing in the drive, weeping. As I stepped out, he rushed over and picked me up. He thought I had changed my mind. He thought I had come back.

But I left. Again.

A year passed, me in Texas, him in Colorado, by that time Boulder, but we never turned away, our approach toward one another like the pull of a river. One day, I found two letters from him in the mail. I drove back to Colorado.

The bearded man and I lasted four years. Four months after our daughter was born, he woke me one morning to say he was going, for good. His sudden absence loomed like the Flatirons. I'd drive every street, looking for nothing but the blue of his truck. I'd leave questions on his voicemail. He never answered.

☙

I should have come back to Boulder years ago. When I left, I left lonely and aching and lost, but when my daughter and I returned, I returned to images I had forgotten, like the photos of her at six months that slipped from a book last week. When I looked up at the balcony of our old apartment, I heard the click-click click-click of my daughter's swing in the living room. When I turned down one street, I saw my friend, Charles, in his black coat, sitting across from me on the patio of the Hotel Boulderado. I drove near the trail I used to run along the foothills. Saw myself laughing as I ducked into the Sink for a pint. Setting the infant seat down in the upstairs ballroom of Boulder Bookstore while I pulled paperbacks from shelves. I passed the day care where I picked up my daughter that day in June after the bearded man stepped onto an elevator, after I moved to a window in the courthouse to watch his blue truck pull out of the parking lot. He left town not long after. No idea where he might be now.

☙

That June, as I sat on this bench with my father, I studied the graph of my life before me—I would raise my daughter on my own. My father patted my knee. We were looking at the Flatirons when he said the words, "It must be hard to leave such a beautiful place."

☙

Finally, the street empties.

"The sights we see and the sounds we hear now have none of the quality of the past," Woolf writes.

I left Boulder a long time ago, and eventually, the sadness left me. I had to come back to see the beauty, the best part of this place. She huddles against me, so much taller than I, her long blonde hair a swirl in the wind. I snap the photograph.

# The Rooms

It's the middle of the night, or maybe it's just dark in my memory. I've already put Indie to bed. She's ten, maybe eleven, and we're living in northern New York. I'm standing in the living room, hitting my palm against a wall and shouting, "Something has to change. Something has to *change*."

Not long ago, I asked Indie if she remembers that night. She said she doesn't. But I can still summon the room, still feel the pinch in my chest. My weariness. At what, I don't remember, but I can guess it was about a late check in the mail or not finding a permanent university position or maybe it was the snow falling outside the window in April.

In our memories, there are rooms we'll always be standing in, saying one thing or another. Or not saying what we should.

In high school, before I had my driver's license, I snuck my father's Olds 98 out of the garage. I wanted to borrow an outfit from my friend Amy, an outfit my mother would never allow. I can still feel the rush of rounding Riggs Circle, the windows down, the radio up. Later, when my parents pulled into the garage in my mother's Cutlass, my father noticed pens and a notebook on his floorboard. I had forgotten to put the seat back (and turn down 97.1 FM, The Eagle). In the living room, I sat on the brick ledge of the fireplace, watching him yell. At fifteen, I was growing more defiant, more confident in my rebellions. "When you leave this house," he raised his arms, "you're going to go wild. Wild!" I stood up, arms by my sides, fists clenched. I yelled back, "I already have!"

By that time, I was a weekend drinker, always going as far and as fast as I could toward oblivion. My escapes were the kind that came from roaming our Texas town and passing a bottle of Boone's Farm in the backseat or giving some guy from geometry class a twenty for ecstasy or roaring beyond the city limits toward the shores of Lake Ray Hubbard.

My curfew was eleven thirty, but I often got around it by spending the night at Amy's. Worse yet, she told her parents she was staying with me. The only connection I had to my parents on those nights was from a pay phone.

When Indie was little, we were poor. I'd often take rolls of toilet paper from the English building. I'd add prices while grocery shopping, Almost daily, I'd divide my checking balance by how many days were left in the month. Sometimes I'd falter under the pressure and yell into the cramped rooms of our apartment. Every time, I'd assure Indie, "I'm not yelling at you. I'm yelling at the world." It wasn't until she was twelve that she finally responded in a sad voice: "It sure sounds like you're yelling at me."

I stopped yelling.

As Indie approached high school, I braced myself for a turn. I readied myself for her own wildness, her rebellions, her yelling at the world and at me. I figured the smokes I'd kept locked in my glove box at her age, the boys who lingered outside my bedroom window, even the Bartles & Jaymes I'd kept in my trunk had set me up for the surge I assumed would come. It never did.

I gave Indie the same curfew, eleven thirty, though I added an "ish," remembering how I used to speed across town to get through the back door on time. More often than not, Indie texts me well before her curfew that she's on her way home.

When she started driving, I told her to text me both when she arrived and when she left. She told me how some of her friends gasped in horror at my rule, while others said they wished their parents cared where they were. Last month, I told her she could stop texting because soon she'll be coming and going from places I don't even know exist a thousand miles away. Just now she texted, "I'm at work!"

My mother and I spoke a jagged language, and sometimes we didn't speak at all. When I was in sixth grade, I told her she was a bad mother. I don't remember why. We were standing in the dining room—I can still see the thick gold carpet, the shine of the dining room table, her tears. I never apologized. I should have.

Those years when we lived in New York, I had a friend whose children were in their twenties. She and I would go on walks through the woods beyond the campus, and once, as we stepped around a fallen tree limb, she said, "Always apologize to your child. If you want a good relationship with her when she's older, say you're sorry when you need to." It was good advice.

In graduate school, one of my professors asked why I never wrote about my daughter, who was barely one at the time. "There's no conflict there," I told her. And so it has gone, all these years. No shouting matches, no slamming doors, no silent treatments.

Indie was only three when I went to rehab. My days had turned into a steady stream of wine. My mother mailed me a letter: "You have a daughter who calls you her best friend. Don't lose that." My father left a message on my voice mail: "Pull your head out of your ass."

I did.

At eighteen, Indie still calls me her best friend.

Maybe she and I have always gotten along because it's the two of us. Or maybe it's because we only have each other. It's tough to turn on that.

Earlier this year, we went to New York City for the first time. I think it was our fourth day of riding subways and staring at maps on our phones and sharing a small hotel room. We were turning onto Forty-Sixth Street from Sixth Avenue just as dusk settled between the buildings. After a long day of walking, we were weary. When Indie said she was tired, that she wanted to get back to our hotel, I stopped. I spun around and shouted into the blur of horns and a passing tour bus.

The days of this last year with her at home are dwindling. Soon so much will have to change.

It had been years since I yelled at the world. And for the first time, my daughter yelled back. We stood in a front of a bodega, stunned. Suddenly the busy street felt like a small room. We dropped our heads and stared at the sidewalk as if we had spilled something. "You know," she said, "we don't have to fight because I'm leaving."

We both said our sorrys. We went on our way.

# Gone

I'm pulling onto I-35 North. It's morning, and Indie, is in the passenger seat. The sky's a soft blue, as if every cloud has somewhere else to be. When I put on my blinker and move into the right lane, Indie tells me that I-35 runs from Laredo, Texas, to Duluth, Minnesota, something she learned last year in school. I ask her how far that is, and she taps her phone. 1,568 miles. Today we're only traveling forty.

Indie and I watch the news at night. We see the empty streets of New York City. We listen to the stories about San Francisco. Texas moves at a slower speed, and the only sign our world is changing is in the empty grocery store shelves. But we feel it coming, especially when Indie worries that all the ceremonies of her senior year will be canceled.

I had a plan, something we could do before we couldn't do it anymore: get in the car and go far enough to leave everything behind, if only for a little while. Last night I asked Indie if she wanted to get up early and get on the road and cross the Oklahoma border. No stops, no gas stations, just there and back. Her face lit up. We set our alarms.

My daughter grew up on highways, I-70 and I-84 and I-90, chatting or slumbering in the passenger seat as we moved from state to state, nine in all. Every time we crossed a border, I'd honk the horn. This highway, I-35, crosses six states. Today we're only crossing one.

I don't like to admit this, but I don't always know what Indie needs when she's upset, when she folds into herself or drives the streets of town with no direction or when I hear a catch in her voice over the phone. In those times, I feel useless and sad and lost.

Last week I was running around the lake when I saw a young woman in a clearing off the path. She had a blue backpack, a dark coat, and lavender hair. Indie put pink highlights in her blonde hair a few weeks ago. I love them. She loves them.

If you grow up always going, it's hard not to want to always be gone.

The sign says twenty-one miles to Gainesville, the last Texas town before the border. Along the way, Indie points to cows in a field, a dilapidated horse ranch, an empty mansion with window frames but no windows. I tell her she can turn on her alt-rock station, but she says what's playing is fine. The Doobie Brothers, "Minute by Minute." We sing along.

On my second pass around the lake, I watched the lavender woman move in circles while a wand hovered in midair around her. She guided it with her hands. Magic, I thought, she's practicing magic.

We're approaching the city limits of Gainesville. I turn down "Sister Golden Hair" to ask Indie where she would go if she could go anywhere. Boston, she says, because she had a layover there when she traveled to her university's visitation day last November, and from her plane window, Boston looked beautiful.

A few days ago, the president of the university she will attend in the fall sent an email with these words: "The campus, at the moment, is absolutely still. The shadows remain long at dusk and dawn, east and west."

Up ahead, we see a large bright sign between the north and south routes of I-35. Oklahoma. I speed up a little. I honk the horn. Indie raises her arms and lets out a long whoop.

In two days, our county will declare a shelter-in-place order. Four days after that, we will be under a stay-at-home order.

But for now, we pass grassy fields and wooden fences, an abandoned single-story motel with diamond-shaped windows, and one gas station after another. My daughter and I talk the way we always do on the road, a conversation that hovers between what we dream and what we remember.

On the way back, I think of the woman in the clearing, her magic wand floating. How I wish she could say the word that would turn back time.

# Summer

# TEXAS HISTORY

The Baker Hotel rose above the Texas trees so straight ahead we didn't trust the turns we were told to take. I pulled off I-20, and Indie read directions from her phone. I took a left, away from the building that loomed like a castle in the distance. It felt as if we were going in the wrong direction, until we turned onto Oak Street. As we got closer to the fourteen-story hotel (abandoned since 1970), we leaned down to marvel at the top-floor balcony, at all those empty rooms towering over the small town of Mineral Wells, fifty miles west of Fort Worth.

The state reopened in May, and the makeshift sign that had been hanging on the side of Applebee's (OPEN TO GO) came down. For forty-nine days before reopening, the state of Texas had been limited to essential businesses, and while the governor declared a statewide emergency, he never issued a formal stay-at-home order. All that time, I only went to the grocery store or 7-Eleven, darting with a Pac-Man savvy down aisles, away from the maskless. Only on July 2, after the reopening of Texas proved to be a disaster, did the governor mandate the wearing of masks.

When Indie began her senior year last fall, she was gone more than she was home—band practice and contests, game nights, working until one a.m. sometimes at her restaurant job, going out with friends, hanging out at their houses. I understood it was a prelude, a slow and increasing separation to prepare us for her leaving. Suddenly we were both at home, navigating a new direction.

It's hard to tell when spring turned to summer, every day the same, and for so many of those days I wondered if Indie's last year at home would turn out not to be the last year at all. But when her university announced in June that they would hold classes on campus in the fall, I wanted to make these very last days something we'd both remember.

We call them half-tank trips, because that's as far as we go, half a tank. We never leave the car, and we're back home within an hour or two. Indie prefers I surprise her with the direction and destination, so it's only after we leave—about once a week—that I tell her where we're headed.

We live forty miles north of Dallas in a town crowded by highways, concrete, and construction. Population: 142,173. The cities we visit hover between one and five thousand, except for Mineral Wells, which is around fifteen.

This summer, we've gone in search of an abandoned motel just north of town (never found it); followed farmland for nineteen miles to Pilot Point, Texas, where the bank robbery scene in *Bonnie and Clyde* was filmed; toured a town nicknamed Gingerbread City for the architecture of its houses; placed silk wisteria flowers on my parents' grave; taken a fifteen-minute drive to the largest mansion in the state; learned the histories of towns as Indie read them from her phone; parked in front a saloon built in 1873, the last stop on the Chisholm Trail before the Red River; we've wondered at empty train depots; pulled into the parking lots of the First United Methodist Churches in Nocona and Pilot Point and Sanger, where my grandfather served as the preacher decades ago. I took photos of all these places from the car, photos that will one day be an archive of the summer Indie left for college.

Indie and I've watched *Ghost Adventures* for years, following Zak Bagans and his crew through abandoned hotels, dusty mansions, and rusty prisons. One episode, "Crazy Town," featured an investigation of the Baker Hotel and one of its ghosts, a woman who fell from the balcony in the thirties.

Opened in 1929, the Baker Hotel boasted four hundred and fifty rooms, two ballrooms, a beauty shop, a bowling alley, a gymnasium, and the first Olympic-size pool in the country. It was a high-class destination in the thirties and forties, but once the interstate system led traffic away from the city in the sixties, the hotel suffered a decline until its closure. The hotel is currently being restored. As we drove around the construction fence, Indie read that Judy Garland stayed in the hotel in 1943 and mailed a letter from the post office up the hill from the hotel.

Rolling through these quiet towns, we note storefront signs: "Please wear a mask." "All Customers Required to Wear a Mask." "No mask, no entrance." And the one we saw on the front of an antique store: "The Governor recommends wearing masks or keeping a 6-foot distance!!!"

What stays with us, sometimes, is not what we expected to find, but what we found instead. Beyond the town square courthouses, the landmarks and landscapes and Fleetwood Mac's *Greatest Hits*, beyond the *Office Ladies* episode for "Casino Night," when we learned it was John Krasinski's first on-screen kiss (Jenna Fischer's second), Indie and I encountered a truth we wouldn't have known as sharply had we not turned through these small pockets of Texas: the 2020 flags promoting a second term.

Could anyone have convinced any of us a year ago of all the turns to come, of all the wrong directions or the way so many would stand up to demand the right ones? Maybe there's never been any such thing as straight ahead.

During what turned out to be our last half-tank trip, Indie received an email from her university: she will have to quarantine for fourteen days in New York before arriving on campus. Driving west, we counted back the days from her move-in date and realized how soon we must leave.

In a few days, Indie and I will begin the cross-country trip on a road we've never traveled, the one that will separate us.

# There Was Beauty

"What is documented, at last, is not the thing itself but the way of seeing—the object infused with the subject."

— Mark Doty

I'm reading the billboards along I-44 East while Indie sleeps in the passenger seat. Today is our second seven-hour drive on our trip to her college in New York. We left Texas Wednesday, and we've made it through Oklahoma and Missouri. Now we're halfway through Indiana, where I pass a sign for foot-high pies. Indie stirs and sits up, tells me she wants to drive.

We talk about that difficult year often now, turn its pages. For years we didn't. Maybe it's because she's leaving, but for the past few weeks we've been trading stories about all the places we've lived, and that one comes up more than the others. What we carry from it.

Over the phone, the landlady had described the couch, the coffee table, and the desk that would be in the basement apartment before we arrived, but the day we opened the door to our new home, we found a twin bed against the wall. For a year, Indie slept on the mattress on the floor, and I slept on an air mattress on top of the box spring. Our small dining table, the only furniture we brought, took up most of the kitchen and became my writing desk.

That year, Indie walked the two blocks to the elementary school on the corner. Sixth grade. I'd go one block with her, then stand on the sidewalk and watch until she stepped through the gate. Back at the house, I'd climb the steps down to the basement to write or prepare for the two classes I taught at a university downtown. The footsteps of the man who rented a room on the first floor were heavy, unsettling. The landlady hadn't mentioned he lived there.

We cross into Ohio, glide through unwavering greenery and billboards for antique stores. Indie passes a flatbed truck stacked with bags of grapefruit. I snap a photo.

On the fifteenth of every month that year, my mother sent me a check to help out, and she sent Indie a small stack of single dollar bills. An hour after we pulled away from that house for the last time, I checked my rearview mirror to make sure the buildings of downtown were miles behind us.

But there was beauty that year: The tree outside our landlady's front yard—she paid me forty dollars a month to buy seed and keep the birdhouses full. All the hours those birds would flit and fly outside the window as I wrote. The sidewalk one morning after Indie and I had taken our nightly walk as she pulled petals from red tulips between our steps. The days we took off for the beach, Indie riding her scooter while I ran behind. The bookstore.

Every time we went, Indie and I'd go straight to a book she found in the children's section. It was Jon Klassen's *I Want My Hat Back*, an illustrated hardcover with a bear on the front. The book begins, "My hat is gone. I want it back." I'd whisper-read while Indie turned the pages. We loved how the bear asks a fox and a frog and a turtle and a rabbit (wearing a red hat) and a snake and some other creature the same question, "Have you seen my hat?" And while none of them claim to have seen the hat (not even the rabbit), our favorite response was the mysterious creature's: "What is a hat?" We'd giggle in the aisle then set the book back on the shelf, sorry to leave it behind.

At the end of that year, we moved to New Mexico, a three-day drive. On the second day, before we left a La Quinta in Amarillo, Texas, Indie gave me my birthday present. It was wrapped in paper that looked like an antique map, along with a note she had written on half a piece of white paper, as if she had carefully torn it down the middle after creasing it. The note was decorated with silly faces and hearts and stick figures (us holding hands) and *I love you*s.

When I pulled back the wrapping paper, there it was—the book with the bear on the cover.

Back home, I keep the book on an end table in our living room. The wrapping paper's still inside, along with Indie's note. I've always thought of the book as a map, an answer to the question, "What is a home?"

As we pass silos and barns, the miles speed by.

# ON LASTS

Summer slips away, like so much else this year. It's late August, midafternoon, and I'm sitting on a porch in upstate New York. This is the final week Indie and I have together on our cross-country trip to her new college. These days are the last ones before we say goodbye at her dorm, before we begin to unfold the pages of our separate lives.

☙

When her senior year began, I decided to keep fresh flowers on her nightstand. I enjoyed choosing different types, different colors, surprising her every week or so with a fresh vase. I thought of the flowers as celebration, but when everything shut down, they felt more like an apology, or an offering of grace. I let her pick out the last ones. They were cream roses, their petals like stationery.

☙

Not long before we left Texas two weeks ago, I asked Indie if she'd like to take me on a tour of her favorite places in high school. She grabbed her keys and drove us to a doughnut store, to the turn she took so many times on Crescent Street, past her school parking space under a tree, to the restaurant where she had worked for over a year, to Sonic Drive-In, space 23, the one she and her best friend pulled into every time, and to the band practice field, telling me stories the whole way. At the Dairy Queen on University, she told me it had the slowest drive-through in town, but the best mint Oreo Blizzards.

☙

At the final custody hearing in Boulder in 2003 (Indie was sixteen months old), the judge ordered the only visitation Indie's father requested (five days every summer). He left the courtroom without a word. My parents had flown in from Texas, and together we watched him walk down the hallway and step into an elevator. As the doors closed, my father said, "Well, you'll never see him again." He was right.

☙

I've long been fascinated with a photo of an abandoned post office in the middle of the Mojave. The blue POST on the small building, the faded OFFICE. The two windows with blinds sun-stained to teal. The wooden door with 90820 painted in red above it. Who was the last person to pull that door closed, to check the lock and make sure?

☙

In college I had an American literature professor who liked to pose the question, "What happens after the last page?" I'd raise my hand to answer, my mind running wild at the idea of what happens *after* an ending.

☙

When Indie was little and it was time to leave—a friend's house or a playground—I'd tell her, "If you don't leave now, you can't come back." I never had to tell her twice. The first time, she understood, was the last time.

☙

I'll always carry the look on Indie's face when she turned to take one last look at our apartment before we began the drive here.

ᴂ

How often I return to *Door Wide Open*, the letters between Kerouac and Johnson that started the year *On the Road* was published. Johnson offers commentary throughout, beginning with the first sentence: "The night of our blind date in January 1957, Jack couldn't even afford to buy me a cup of coffee—his last twenty had vanished earlier that day when he'd bought a pack of cigarettes and received change for a five, so I treated him to a hot dog and baked beans at Howard Johnson's." I tell my students they can often find an entire work in its opening line, and sometimes even the ending.

ᴂ

Last October, Indie and I went to the State Fair of Texas on the last day. We followed the route my father had taken us on every year—Fletcher's Corn Dogs, the automobile building, the Midway for Skee-Ball, the food building for a bag of malt balls, a ride through the haunted house with the cars that swoop down a hill (my father, in his ball cap, always whooped on the way down). We did everything he had loved to do, along with giving our leftover game tickets to a family with small children on our way out.

This fall, there will be no fair.

ᴂ

As we've been driving across the country, we've seen CLASS OF 2020 signs on barns and marquees, once on a large rock in the Adirondacks. This year has given us all unexpected conclusions.

How many lasts came and went without our knowing? And how many lasts slipped away?

☙

We're quarantining at an Airbnb, our final stop before the four-hour drive to Indie's campus. There's a nice breeze on the porch today. A few houses down, a man mows his lawn.

Every night here, we've been watching a movie we loved when Indie was little (last night, *Fantastic Mr. Fox*). When the movie's over, I come out here and listen to Jackson Browne. I've always loved the last lines of "These Days," when the singer tells someone not to confront him about his failures because there's no need, he hasn't forgotten them.

☙

It turns out the last thing I bought my mother was a vanilla bean frozen coffee. She had never had one, and when she took a sip, she looked over at the nurse with joy: "It tastes like snow ice cream!"

☙

Every time I've moved, I've pretended the last time I see people is not that at all.

See you tomorrow.

See you soon.

I can't bear to say goodbye.

☙

I never leave behind the last sip when I drink wine in a restaurant. Yesterday, Indie told me she'll miss sitting across from me in a booth, talking while I finish my wine.

☙

"Everything that happens is the last time it happens."

—Sarah Manguso

☙

Earlier, the scent of rain was sudden. I looked up to see clouds fold away the last bit of sun like an envelope. The breeze cooled. And then a falling so quiet I had to stare at the trees to see the drops.

I threw open the screen door and called out to Indie. She ran outside, and we stood on the steps, watching a rain that reminded me of the beaded curtains we once had in a kitchen doorframe, several homes and years ago.

I already know the last thing I'm going to say to her.

This isn't the last essay in this series, but it's the last one I'll write while Indie's in the next room.

# RETURN

Every time I leave for a trip, I imagine its ending. After zipping up my suitcase and rolling it to the door, I turn to look at the empty rooms. The closed blinds, the couch pillows, the dark kitchen. I close the door, picturing the day I'll come back and turn the key, set my suitcase inside, and flip on the kitchen light. How ordinary those moments of return always feel.

☙

Endings come suddenly when you don't let yourself think about them. Like a train pulling away from a station, picking up speed faster than you can bear.

☙

On Move-In Day, parents weren't allowed inside the dorms because of Covid precautions, and each student was given a fifteen-minute window to get their belongings inside and say goodbye. Indie made one trip after another up the steps to her room, carrying suitcases and storage bins, while I unloaded her car, trying not to stare at all the goodbyes in the parking lot.

I saw a mother on her tiptoes clinging to her son's neck, a father handing his daughter a twenty (something my father had done in that moment), everyone taking turns giving long hugs. Then the parents climbed into their cars and pulled off their masks to wipe away tears. When a lanky young man suddenly turned on the sidewalk to wave at his parents as they drove away, I looked up at the trees and blinked back tears. Within minutes, it would be my turn to drive away.

☙

When I was in graduate school in my late twenties, there was a bar across from the English building. Every time I hung out there, I'd punch the numbers for Jackson Browne's "Running on Empty" on the jukebox.

I think we all have places we wish we could stand again so that we might know who we were, or even weren't, in them, or to finally feel the distance between that person and the person we are now. If I could stand in front of that jukebox next to the girl I was then, would I even tell her how "that road turned into the road I'm on"? Or would I just sit in a booth in the corner, tap my foot, and listen to the song?

☙

After leaving Indie at her dorm, I drove a rental car to the airport. Sitting at a corner gas station across from campus, I had to tell my foot to press on the gas, to *go*. I took the winding route through the North Country while Pandora played all my seventies favorites—Firefall, America, Bread—as if I had programmed the soundtrack. At certain songs, I'd glance over at the empty passenger seat, where Indie wasn't, from where she's always sung along. Two hours later, when I took the airport exit, Jackson Browne came on and carried me the rest of the way, singing about running and running and never being able to get away from himself.

☙

Right now it feels like a part of me will always be standing on the sidewalk outside Indie's dorm, cupping her face with my hands to say the last thing, then watching her disappear through the propped-open door. I suspect that years from now, I'll write about standing on that sidewalk, and I'll have the words for what's impossible for me to know now.

☙

Not long before Indie left, she bought me a step stool so that I could reach the top cabinets in the kitchen, something she's always done for me.

☙

The other night, after my friends picked me up from the airport and dropped me off at my apartment, I turned the key, opened the door, and rolled my suitcase inside. It was only then that I realized I had not turned to look at the empty rooms as we were leaving them. I had not pictured the moment I would come back to them alone.

☙

Yesterday morning Indie texted to ask if I wanted to FaceTime so she could show me her room and take me on a tour of her dorm. You'd think Brad Pitt had texted me.

☙

The first trip to the grocery store after I got back was the hardest.

☙

Since childhood, I've slept with a fan in my room, either a ceiling fan or an oscillating one, but I haven't used one in years, afraid I wouldn't hear Indie if she cried or called out. I'm going to buy a fan today.

☙

I haven't lived alone since I was in my late twenties. Last month, I turned fifty. In many ways, it feels like a pause button's been released, and I can return to thinking, for the first time in a long time, about who I am—beyond a mother.

# Gratitude

The first thank you goes to Nadja Spiegelman, former Online Editor for *The Paris Review Daily*, who commissioned the original four-season series of essays for a column, *The Last Year,* in 2019-2020. I couldn't have imagined a better editor for this project. You made me feel that the essays, their meaning and purpose, were as important to you as they were to me.

Thank you to Krista Stevens, who published "Road Grad" a year later in *Longreads.*

To Jill McCabe Johnson, amazing Editor-in-Chief of Wandering Aengus Press, I'm grateful that you reached out and convinced me that WAP was the right press to publish these essays as a book. Thank you for your beautiful book design, cover to cover. Another thanks for pairing me with the wonderful Ana Maria Spagna, a kind and insightful editor who respected the original versions of the essays while opening them up in just the right places. Ana Maria, my respect for you abounds.

Thank you, Charles Blackstone. You've been with Indie and me all along. We consider you family.

Here's to good people and friends who Indie and I met along the way and who will always be a part of our lives and our memories: Brian Flota, Ray, David Lazar, the late William Bradley, Mark Slouka and his family, the Huntley family, Kim Garza, Clinton Crockett Peters, Gabe Montesanti and Kelly Bresnahan, and Amanda and Kevin Yanowski.

A special thank you to Carol Howard and Linda Hammonds, lifelong friends of my mother's, who always show Indie and me so much love.

Always, I am thankful to and for Indie, who had no idea I was writing these essays during that year and who, when I told her about them two years later, said, "It's too soon for me to read them. I want to keep my own memories for now." Here's to all the memories I didn't write about here, Indie, all the ones only you and I know and all the ones that have made us who we are—to ourselves, to each other.

# About the Author

Jill Talbot is the author of *The Way We Weren't: A Memoir* (Soft Skull) and *Loaded: Women and Addiction* (Seal Press), co-editor of *The Art of Friction: Where (Non)Fictions Come Together* (U of Texas Press), and editor of *Metawritings: Toward a Theory of Nonfiction* (Iowa), as well as the forthcoming craft book *The Essay Form(s)* from Columbia University Press. She is the winner of *The Florida Review*'s 2021 Jeanne Leiby Chapbook Award Winner for her short story collection, *A Distant Town.* Her writing has appeared in journals such as *AGNI*, *Brevity*, *Colorado Review*, *Diagram*, *Gulf Coast*, *Hotel Amerika*, *The Paris Review Daily*, and *The Rumpus* and has been recognized six times in *The Best American Essays.* She is Associate Professor of Creative Writing and University Distinguished Teaching Professor at the University of North Texas.

CPSIA information can be obtained
at www.ICGtesting.com
Printed in the USA
JSHW070718070723
44048JS00007B/144